Biomes
of North
America

A Journey into a River

by Rebecca L. Johnson

with illustrations by Phyllis V. Saroff

 Carolrhoda Books, Inc./Minneapolis

Carolrhoda Books, Inc.
A division of Lerner Publishing Group
241 First Avenue North
Minneapolis, Minnesota 55401 U.S.A.

Website address: www.lernerbooks.com

Library of Congress Cataloging-in-Publication Data

Johnson, Rebecca L.
    A journey into a river / by Rebecca L. Johnson ; illustrations by
Phyllis V. Saroff.
      p.   cm. — (Biomes of North America)
    Includes index.
    Summary: Takes readers on a journey into a river, showing
examples of how the animals and plants are connected and
dependent on each other and the river's freshwater environment.
    ISBN: 1-57505-595-3 (lib. bdg. : alk. paper)
    1. Stream ecology—Juvenile literature. 2. Rivers—Juvenile
literature. [1. Stream ecology. 2. Rivers. 3. Ecology.] I. Saroff,
Phyllis V., ill. II. Title. III. Series.
QH541.5.S7J65 2004
577.6'4—dc22   2003015727

Manufactured in the United States of America
1 2 3 4 5 6 - JR - 09 08 07 06 05 04

Words
to Know

BANK—the land along the sides of a river or stream

CURRENT—a flow of water in a particular direction

DEN—a hole in which an animal lives or raises its young

FINS—fanlike parts that stick out from the body of a fish. Fins help a fish swim and balance in the water.

FOOD CHAIN—the connection among living things that shows what eats what in an ecosystem

GILLS—organs animals such as fish and tadpoles use to "breathe" underwater

GRAVITY—the force that pulls objects toward the center of the earth

LARVAE (LAR-vee)—preadult forms of some kinds of insects

NOCTURNAL (nahk-TUHR-nuhl)—active at night

NYMPHS (NIHMFS)—preadult forms of some kinds of insects

PREDATOR (PREH-duh-tur)—an animal that hunts and eats other animals

PREY (PRAY)—an animal that is hunted and eaten by other animals

SCALES—the thin, flat, hard plates that cover and protect the skin of certain kinds of fish

SOURCE—the place where a river or stream begins

STREAM—a flow of water

TALONS (TAL-uhns)—an eagle's large, sharp claws

WATER BIOME (BYE-ohm)—a major community of living things in a water-based area, such as a lake or river

Sparkling water

flowing swiftly by

A furry head with long whiskers pops up from behind a fern. After a moment, a young otter steps out from her hiding place and scampers toward the water. It's clear and cold and flowing fast. In one graceful motion, the otter slides down the wet bank and slips into the river.

Fast or slow, the water in a river is always moving.

A river is a ribbon of water that weaves its way over the land. It is constantly moving and changing. Ripples and swirls and tiny whirlpools dance endlessly across its surface. The water murmurs and chuckles to itself as the river hurries on its way.

You can find rivers on every continent and all but the tiniest islands. Some rivers are small—hardly more than streams. Others are big and broad and deep.

Some rivers twist back and forth across the landscape like silvery snakes. Some carve paths through deep canyons. Some even plunge off steep cliffs to form waterfalls that can catch sunbeams and turn them into rainbows.

Rivers carve out canyons (above) *and form waterfalls* (left) *as they flow across the landscape.*

7

Chances are you've seen a river—or a stream, which can join with other streams to form a river. Maybe you've seen a lake or a wetland too. If you live near the coast, you may have walked along the edge of the ocean or an estuary. An estuary forms where the freshwater of a river meets the salty water of the ocean.

Rivers, along with lakes, wetlands, estuaries, and the ocean, make up the earth's water biomes. A water biome is a water-based region that is home to a unique group of living things. They are all adapted, or specially suited, to living in that place.

Water biomes range from still mountain lakes (top) *and boggy wetlands* (middle) *to the vast ocean* (bottom) *that encircles the earth.*

Each biome's living things, from tiny microscopic creatures to large plants and animals, form a community. Each member of that community depends on the other members. All these living things, in turn, depend on the water—fresh or salty, moving or still—that forms their watery home. They swim through it, find food in it, and are sometimes carried from place to place by it. Without the water, they could not survive.

A fish catches an insect in a shallow lake (above). A raccoon that lives in a wetland eats a crayfish (left).

Where does the water in a river come from? The water in many mountain rivers comes from melting snow and ice. Other rivers are fed by springs, where water comes bubbling up from deep underground. Rainwater flows off the land to fill rivers too.

Melting mountain glaciers feed a river in Alaska (right). Water bubbles up from underground at a river's source in Missouri (below).

A drought may slowly dry a river up (above), while heavy rains can turn it into a raging torrent (below).

During dry spells, a river's water level may drop. If the water gets low enough, parts of the river bottom are exposed.

Heavy rains or melting snow can make a river swell. So much water may be added that the river overflows its banks. An overflowing river floods the land around it.

11

Because of gravity, water flows downhill. Where the land is steep, rivers move very fast. As the water rushes along, it is churned into foaming rapids and stinging spray. Where the land is flatter, rivers move at a lazier pace.

Rivers begin in all sorts of places. Small rivers join to form larger ones. These may stretch for thousands of miles until they reach the sea.

River water may start its downhill journey high in the mountains (above), but it eventually flows into the ocean (right).

Fast or slow, narrow or broad, short or long—
rivers are full of life. But much of that life is hidden
beneath the swirling surface of the water.

    The otter has returned. Water streams off her
thick fur as she climbs back up the bank. And
look—the otter is not alone. She's been joined by
her brother. Let's follow these two otters on a
journey into the river.

With their wet fur shimmering in the sun, two otters nuzzle each other on the riverbank.

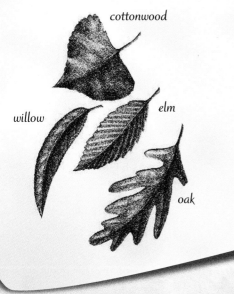

cottonwood

willow

elm

oak

Tall trees grow close together on either side of the river.

Here on the bank, the air smells like damp soil and green growing things. There's a cool breeze coming off the river. The water makes soft, gurgling sounds as it rushes past. If you put your hand in the river, you'd feel it pushing hard. This movement of the water is called the current.

Trees crowd both riverbanks. Their branches arch over the water, like scraggly arms reaching for the other side. The tallest trees are cottonwoods, with fluttering gray green leaves. Willows, elms, and oaks stand among them.

Other kinds of plants grow beneath the trees. There are bushy dogwoods and feathery ferns. Jack-in-the-pulpits nestle in the shadows. Violets' pale purple flowers share space with patches of velvety moss.

The leaves of trees and other green plants growing along the river soak up sunshine. The plants use the energy in sunlight to make their own food. Plants, in turn, are food for many kinds of animals. They are a first link in the river's food chain.

Along the riverbank, ferns hug the ground (top) while jack-in-the-pulpits (middle) and violets (below) bloom in the shade.

15

A swallow's small, pointed beak is ideally shaped for snatching flying insects.

The nest holes of bank swallows dot the steep riverbank *(above)*. Swallows peek out of the entrances of their cool underground homes *(inset)*.

Bank swallows swoop back and forth across the river. They are catching mosquitoes and other flying insects to eat. Bank swallows nest in holes that they dig in the sides of steep riverbanks.

The otters live along the bank too. Their home is an underground den. The entrance to the den is hidden by some gnarled tree roots and a thick clump of ferns.

The otters are playing in the shallow water at the river's edge. They wrestle and nip at each other's ears. When one dives, the other follows, like children playing tag. Then they bob to the surface and start the game again.

But playing hard makes the otters hungry. With a final splash, they swim away from the land. The current tugs at their slim, strong bodies as they head downstream.

Webs of skin between an otter's toes aid in swimming.

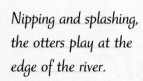

Nipping and splashing, the otters play at the edge of the river.

Dragonflies, stone flies, and long-tailed mayflies all hatch from eggs as larvae or nymphs that eventually change into adult forms.

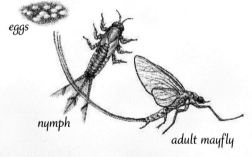

eggs

nymph

adult mayfly

Despite their small size, stone fly larvae are scary-looking predators with powerful legs and huge jaws.

A few feet from the bank, the water is still fairly shallow. The otters can see the river bottom as they swim along. It is made up of small pebbles and sand.

Stone fly nymphs lurk among the pebbles. So do dragonfly nymphs. One day soon, these young insects will leave the water and change into adults with wings.

But for now, these small underwater predators prowl the shallows for food. They eat other insects, tiny fish, and anything else they can catch in their sharp, pinching jaws.

18

Some of the "pebbles" on the river bottom are caddis fly larvae. These insects glue together sand grains and tiny pebbles to make hard cases around their soft bodies. The larvae rely on this clever disguise to avoid being eaten.

When danger threatens, a caddis fly larva pulls back into its case and uses its hard head to block the opening.

Safe inside its armored case of sticks, a caddis fly larva munches on a dead leaf.

19

Underwater plants grow along the shallow edges of the river. Their roots are anchored firmly in the river bottom. Their long, frilly stems sway gently in the current like green ribbons.

Snails crawl slowly up and down the plants. Some are no bigger than a grain of rice. Their spiral shells shimmer in the sunlight.

Spiral-shelled snails (above) crawl along the river bottom and up and down the stems of underwater plants, such as this hornwort (right).

Like a fish, a tadpole uses gills to "breathe" underwater. As it grows into a frog, gills are lost as lungs form.

gills

Pudgy frog tadpoles wriggle through the miniature forest of underwater plants. They dart from one hiding place to another, powered by their long tails.

Frog tadpoles devour tender plants sprouting from the riverbed.

Frogs often anchor their eggs to underwater plants so they aren't swept away by the current.

Frog eggs (dark circles) are surrounded by a thick coat of rubbery "jelly."

The tadpoles hatched from eggs laid by adult frogs. At first, there were thousands of tiny tadpoles in the shallows. But many have been eaten by stone fly nymphs, dragonfly nymphs, small fish, and other predators.

The surviving tadpoles are getting bigger and starting to change. They are losing their tails and sprouting legs. Eventually, they will hop out of the water as young frogs, ready to start a new life on land.

With its eyes placed on top of its head, a frog can be almost completely underwater and still see what is happening around it.

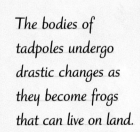

The bodies of tadpoles undergo drastic changes as they become frogs that can live on land.

Two eastern newts rest along the riverbank on a soft carpet of moss.

Salamanders and newts live along the edge of the river too. Like frogs, they started life in the water as tadpoles. Now they scurry about the damp riverbank, looking for insects, worms, and spiders to eat.

As the otters paddle along, they pass over a sculpin. The little fish has its fins braced against small rocks on the river bottom to keep from being swept away by the current.

The sculpin's scaly skin is a mix of browns and grays. It blends in with the colors of the river bottom. As long as it doesn't move, it's easily overlooked. The otters don't see it and keep on swimming.

Superb swimmers, otters move with ease through the water (above). Even the big eyes of a sculpin (left) are colored to help it blend into the river bottom.

25

A kingfisher's nest is built deep into the side of a riverbank.

The kingfisher is a sharp-eyed hunter with a distinctive crest of feathers on its head.

Rat-ta-tat-ta-tat-ta-tat. That's the rattling call of a kingfisher. Here it comes, flying fast along the river. Bright blue feathers flash as the bird lands on a branch that overhangs the water.

With sharp eyes, the kingfisher scans the river. It notices the otters gliding past. But the bird is looking for swirls and shadows made by fish swimming close to the surface.

At that moment, the sculpin swims up to eat an insect that has landed on the water's surface. The kingfisher spots the movement. The bird swoops down and plunges headfirst into the river. It rises from the water with the sculpin wriggling in its beak.

Held tightly in the kingfisher's strong beak, the little fish is about to become dinner.

Otters can see well underwater (left).
A crayfish clambers across the river bottom on spindly, pincer-tipped legs (below).

Farther downstream, the otters are diving for dinner too. They are out in the middle of the river, where the current is fast and strong.

The otters tuck their heads and dive. With their webbed feet, they kick down through the water. On the river bottom, the otters poke their whiskered noses between big rocks. Otters eat mostly fish. But a crayfish would make a tasty appetizer!

The otters cruise past a snapping turtle that is swimming slowly, just above the river bottom. Snapping turtles have sharp, hooked beaks that they use to snare fish and other river dwellers. Once a snapping turtle clamps down on something, it rarely lets go. The otters keep their distance.

Baby turtles hatch from leathery-shelled eggs laid on land by the mother turtle.

A large snapping turtle moves slowly upstream against the current, gripping the rocks with sharp claws.

Where a river runs fairly straight, the water is deepest in the middle.

Catfish get their name from the "whiskers" — called barbels — on their faces.

One of the otters rises to the surface to breathe. She gulps in air, then dives again, down to the deepest part of the river.

Her brother has spotted a catfish hiding under a sunken tree trunk. Catfish spend most of their time near the river bottom. This one's body is covered with streaked and spotted scales that help it blend in with rocks, logs, and mud. The otters eat catfish. But this one is out of reach.

The river is home to many other kinds of fish too. There are bluegills and creek chub. There are small-mouthed bass and lots of trout.

A big bluegill cruises past (left) while a creek chub (below) stays close to rocks and water plants that offer protection from predators.

In some rivers, trout share their home with prehistoric-looking paddlefish. Taste buds on the underside of the paddlefish's snout help it find food.

Unless it moves, a trout is hard to spot against the river's rocky bottom.

Trout are hunters with strong, streamlined bodies. They often hang quietly in the water, facing upstream. They wait for insects and small fish to come downstream with the current. When a potential meal gets close enough, trout strike with lightning speed.

Not far from the catfish, a cutthroat trout is swimming slowly upstream. It spots a big grasshopper that has fallen into the river. With a flick of its powerful tail, the trout zooms to the surface. The grasshopper disappears into the big fish's mouth.

The trout closes in on the unfortunate grasshopper.

The trout has excellent eyesight. It constantly watches for danger in the surrounding water. But it keeps an eye on what's happening above the water too. Trout can see raccoons, bobcats, and other fish-eating animals moving along the riverbank or flying over the water.

Both raccoons (top) and bobcats (right) will work hard—and even get wet—for a tasty meal of trout.

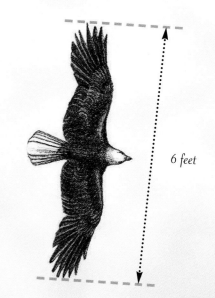

A bald eagle's wingspan is about 6 feet (roughly the height of a tall man).

6 feet

The cutthroat trout sees the bald eagle coming up the river. The eagle soars silently on broad, dark wings. Bald eagles have hooked beaks and huge talons that are as sharp as daggers—perfect for grabbing fish out of the water.

From high above the river, the bald eagle spots the trout. It folds back its wings and dives with its talons outstretched.

The bald eagle swoops down toward the water's surface.

35

An otter's pointed teeth are good for slicing and tearing the meat it eats.

The otter sniffs her just-caught fish while shaking water from her dense fur.

The eagle strikes the water's surface. But the trout is too fast. With an angry cry, the eagle rises with empty claws.

The trout doesn't notice one of the otters closing in from behind. Sharp teeth sink into shiny scales. The otter bobs to the surface with her prize.

Holding the fish high, the otter swims toward the riverbank. As she splashes through the shallows, a water boatman rows madly to get out of the way.

The water boatman is a small water bug, less than an inch long. It uses its long, powerful back legs like oars to move through the water.

For such a small insect, a water boatman has a big appetite. It will attack animals its own size—or larger.

Up on the muddy riverbank, the otter is joined by her brother. Together they settle down to eat.

In the mud around them are tracks made by a mink that lives along this stretch of the river. Like the otters, the mink loves fish. It also eats insects, birds, crayfish, mice—even rabbits.

But you won't see the mink at this time of day. It is fast asleep in a hole in the riverbank. Being nocturnal, it won't come out to hunt until the sun goes down.

A mink's feet are webbed like those of otters. It also has sharp claws for climbing trees and slippery rocks.

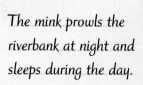

The mink prowls the riverbank at night and sleeps during the day.

Green-backed herons usually feed right at the water's edge (left). *A mother green-backed heron watches over her chicks* (below).

Close by, however, other animals are wide awake and keeping an eye on the otters. A green-backed heron peers out from a tuft of weeds. The greenish blue feathers on his head and back glint in the sunlight.

In a nearby tree, his mate stands up in her nest to get a better look at the otters. Tiny heads poke out from beneath the mother bird. Two sleepy chicks blink in the bright light.

A muskrat lodge is made of twigs. A hole outside the lodge leads to a snug inner chamber.

The muskrat crouches on the bank, wet from a swim in the river.

Farther up the bank, a furry muskrat nibbles tender twigs. Muskrats are plant eaters that spend a lot of time in the water. They build homes out of grasses and small branches along quiet bends in the river.

The muskrat has nothing to fear from the otters, though. And they are too busy eating to notice it.

Farther back from the river's edge, a big elk stands quietly in the shadow of a tall tree. It sniffs the air and then walks down the bank toward the water. Like the muskrat, it isn't afraid of the otters. But the breeze brings the scent of another, much larger hunter.

The elk comes to the river for a long, cool drink.

A coyote can hear the slightest sound with its huge ears. Big padded feet are good for sneaking up on prey.

The coyote sees the otters on the riverbank.

A big coyote has appeared on the riverbank. Her nose twitches as she smells the elk, the muskrat, the otters—and the trout.

The coyote moves in silently on well-padded feet. She creeps closer and closer, until she's just a few feet from the otters. She crouches down in the grass and tenses the muscles in her long legs. Then she springs, just a blur of fur and teeth.

With every muscle tensed, the coyote is ready to spring.

Safe inside their snug den, young coyote pups wait for their mother to return.

At the last moment, the otters see the coyote coming. They dash down the bank and dive into the river.

The coyote watches the otters swim away. Then she picks up the half-eaten fish in her mouth and trots off to her den. The den is high on a distant hillside, where four hungry pups are waiting to be fed.

From the safety of the water, the otters watch the coyote scamper up the riverbank. Their dinner is gone. But the river is full of fish. Together, the otters turn into the swift current and swim off in search of another meal.

With a last look back, the otters continue their hunt for food in the river.

for further
Information
about Rivers

Books

Arnold, Caroline. *Bobcats.* Minneapolis: Lerner Publications Company, 1997.

Donnelly, Andrew. *Waterfalls.* Chanhassen, MN: Child's World, 1999.

Duden, Jane. *Floods! Rising, Raging Waters.* Logan, IA: Perfection Learning, 1999.

Esbensen, Barbara Juster. *Playful Slider: The North American River Otter.* New York: Little Brown & Co, 1993.

Grimm, Phyllis W. *Crayfish.* Minneapolis: Lerner Publications Company, 2001.

Kite, L. Patricia. *Raccoons.* Minneapolis: Lerner Publications Company, 2004.

Miller, Sara Swan. *Frogs and Toads: The Leggy Leapers.* New York: Franklin Watts, 2000.

Rapp, Valerie. *Life in a River.* Minneapolis: Lerner Publications Company, 2003.

Sayre, April Pulley. *River and Stream.* New York: Twenty-First Century Books, 1996.

Staub, Frank. *Herons.* Minneapolis: Lerner Publications Company, 1997.

Wilcox, Charlotte. *Bald Eagles.* Minneapolis: Carolrhoda Books Inc., 2003.

Winner, Cherie. *Coyotes.* Minneapolis: Carolrhoda Books Inc., 1995.

———. *Salamanders.* Minneapolis: Carolrhoda Books Inc., 1993.

———. *Trout.* Minneapolis: Carolrhoda Books Inc., 1998.

Websites

American Rivers—for Kids and Teachers < http://www.amrivers.org/kids/ >

The American Rivers website has information on how rivers are born, the water cycle, food chains, and more, plus games and experiments.

Geography Action! Rivers 2001
< http://www.nationalgeographic.com
/geographyaction/rivers/ >

Follow the flow as the National
Geographic Society takes you on an
interactive tour of a river.

River Otters
< http://www.nationalgeographic.com
/kids/creature_feature/0006/otters.html >

The National Geographic Society's
river otter page has fun facts, an otter
video, otter sounds, and a map of
where otters live. You can even send a
river otter postcard to your friends.

Rivers and Streams
< http://mbgnet.mobot.org/fresh/rivers
/index.htm >

Find out how a stream becomes a river,
meet a variety of river creatures, and
more.

Photo Acknowledgments

The photographs in this book are used with the
permission of: VISUALS UNLIMITED [© Henry
W. Robison, pp. 4–5; © Leonard Lee Rue III,
p. 5 (inset); © Cheyenne Rouse, p. 6; © M. Long,
p. 7 (top); © Jim Hughes, p. 7 (bottom); © Rob &
Ann Simpson, pp. 8 (middle), 31 (bottom), 45
(inset); © Scott Berner, p. 8 (bottom); © Gary
Meszaros, pp. 9 (top), 18, 19, 28 (bottom); © Joe
McDonald, pp. 9 (bottom), 29, 31 (top), 34 (both),
36; © Albert J. Copley, p. 10 (top); © Richard
Thom, p. 10 (bottom); © Bruce Clendenning,
p. 11 (bottom); © Walt Anderson, p. 11 (top);
© Ann B. Swengel, p. 12 (top); © William J.
Weber, p. 12 (bottom); © Ken Lucas-Photo,
p. 13; © Nada Pecnik, p. 15 (middle); © Robert
W. Dom, p. 15 (bottom); © Richard C. Johnson,
p. 16 (main); © Wm. Grenfell, p. 16 (inset); © R.
Al Simpson, p. 21; © John Serrao, p. 22; © David
Wrobel, p. 24; © Glenn Oliver, pp. 25 (bottom),
37; © Wally Eberhart, p. 26; © Gary C. Will,
p. 27; © Gary W. Carter, p. 28 (top); © John G.
Shedd Aquarium, p. 30; © Bill Banaszewski,
p. 32; © Jack Milchanowski, p. 35; © John
Gerlach, p. 38; © Marc Epstein, p. 39 (top);
© Tom Ulrich, p. 40; © Elizabeth Delaney, p. 44;
© Ray Dove, p. 45 (main)]; © USDA Forest
Service, p. 8 (top); © James P. Rowan, pp. 14, 15
(top); © Tom and Pat Leeson, pp. 17, 42, 43;
PHOTO RESEARCHERS [© Millard H. Sharp,
p. 20 (top); © E. R. Degginger, p. 20 (bottom);
© Gary Meszaros, p. 23; © Gregory K. Scott,
p. 39 (bottom); © Renee Lynn, p. 41]; CORBIS
[© Galen Rowell, p. 25 (top); © Dale C. Spartas,
p. 33].

Cover photographs © Brian P. Foss/Visuals
Unlimited (river/background) and © Makonny
T. Titlow/Visuals Unlimited (otter/foreground).

Index

Numbers in **bold** refer to photos and drawings.